P9-DEL-183

SCIENCE EXPLORER
JUNIOR
JUNIOR SCIENTISTS
Experiment with Bugs
by Susan H. Gray

NOTE TO PARENTS AND TEACHERS: Please review the instructions for these experiments before your children do them. Be sure to help them with any experiments you do not think they can safely conduct on their own.

NOTE TO KIDS: Be sure to ask an adult for help with these experiments. Always put your safety first!

Published in the United States of America by Cherry Lake Publishing
Ann Arbor, Michigan
www.cherrylakepublishing.com

Content Editor: Robert Wolffe, EdD, Professor of Teacher Education, Bradley University, Peoria, Illinois
Reading Adviser: Cecilia Minden-Cupp, PhD, Literacy Consultant

Design and Illustration: The Design Lab

Photo Credits: Page 11, ©Joseph Calev/Shutterstock, Inc.; page 15, ©David Lee/Shutterstock, Inc.; page 16, ©Morgan Lane Photography/ Shutterstock, Inc.; page 28, ©EW CHEE GUAN/Shutterstock, Inc.; page 29, ©iStockphoto.com/JLBarranco

Library of Congress Cataloging-in-Publication Data
Gray, Susan Heinrichs.
Junior scientists. Experiment with bugs / by Susan H. Gray.
p. cm.—(Science explorer junior)
Includes bibliographical references and index.
ISBN-13: 978-1-60279-842-7 (lib. bdg.)
ISBN-10: 1-60279-842-7 (lib. bdg.)
1. Wood lice (Crustaceans)—Experiments—Juvenile literature. 2. Worms—Experiments—Juvenile literature. I. Title. II. Title: Experiment with bugs. III. Series.
QL444.M34G73 2010
595.7078–dc22 2009048816

Portions of the text have previously appeared in *Super Cool Science Experiments: Bugs* published by Cherry Lake Publishing.

Cherry Lake Publishing would like to acknowledge the work of The Partnership for 21st Century Skills. Please visit *www.21stcenturyskills.org* for more information.

Printed in the United States of America
Corporate Graphics Inc.
July 2010
CLFA07

TABLE OF CONTENTS

Let's Experiment!

Have you ever done a science **experiment**? They can be lots of fun! You can use experiments to learn about almost anything.

This book will help you learn how to think like a scientist. Scientists have a special way of learning new things. Some people call it the Scientific Method. This is how it often works:

- Scientists notice things. They **observe** the world around them. They ask questions about things they see, hear, taste, touch, or smell. They come up with problems they would like to solve.

- They gather information. They use what they already know to guess the answers to their questions. This kind of guess is called a **hypothesis**.

- Then they test their ideas. They perform **experiments** or build models. They watch and write down what happens. They learn from each new test.

- They think about what they learned and reach a **conclusion**. This means they come up with an answer to their question. Sometimes they **conclude** that they need to do more experiments!

We will think like scientists to learn more about bugs. Insects, worms, and spiders can be found in many different places. Have you ever wondered about these creepy crawlers? Where do they like to live? What kind of weather do they like?

We can answer these questions by doing experiments. Each experiment will teach us something new. Are you ready to be a scientist?

EXPERIMENT #1

Damp or Dry?

What do you do when you are afraid? Roly-poly bugs roll up into balls when they sense danger.

You'll need to find some of these little bugs. Go outside and turn over some large rocks. Do you see any roly-polys? Look under old logs or flowerpots. Use a spoon to scoop them up. Be gentle! Keep them in a plastic tub with damp soil, tree bark, and crushed leaves. Ask an adult to poke some air holes in the tub's lid. Keep the lid on the tub.

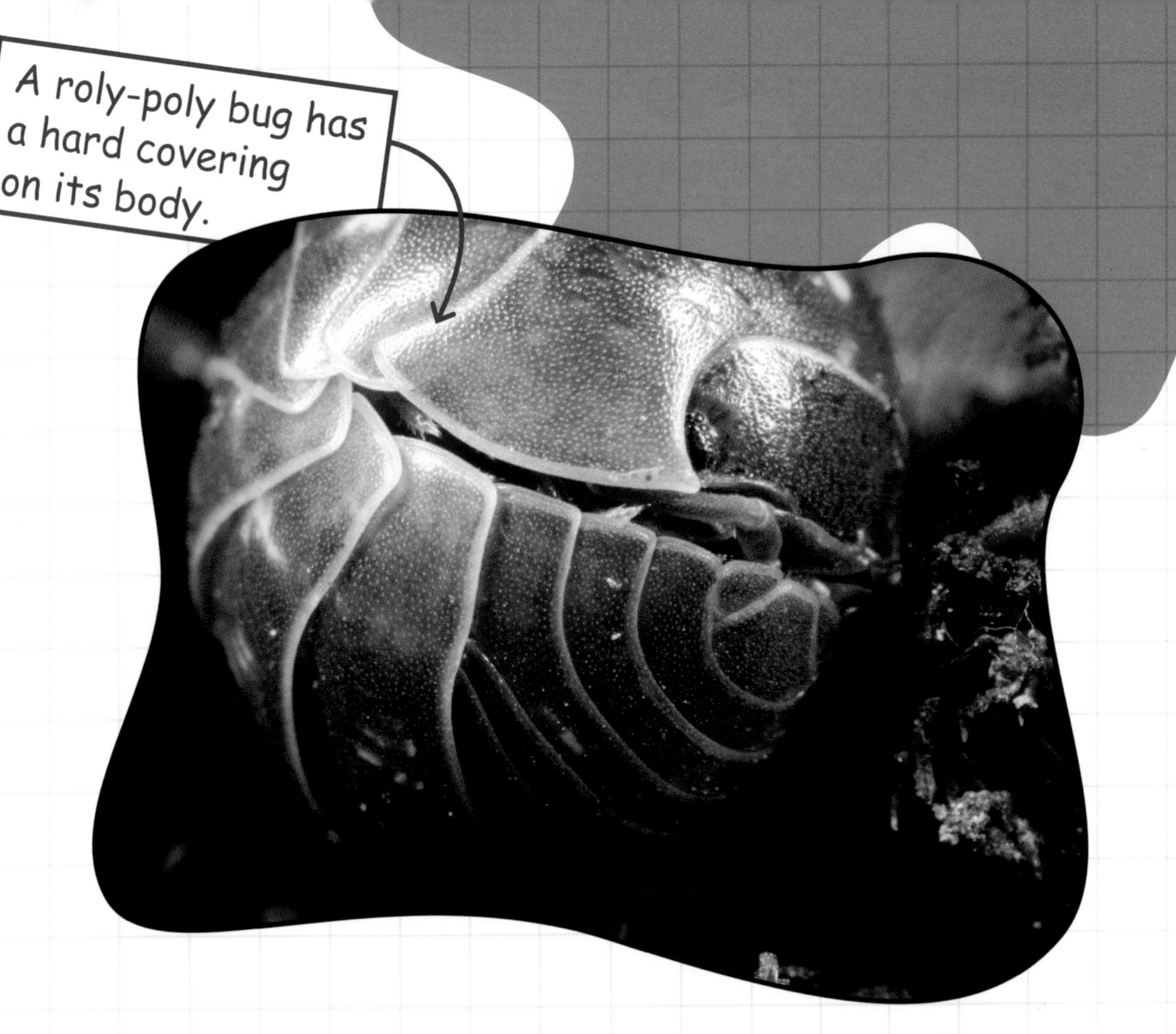

Where did you find the most bugs? Are these places damp or dry? Do you think it matters to these bugs where they live? Let's do an experiment to find out!

First, we need a hypothesis. Here are two choices:

1. Roly-polys would rather live in damp places.
2. Roly-polys do not care where they live.

Here is an experiment to help you test your hypothesis.

Here's what you'll need:

- 8–10 crushed, dry, dead leaves
- Dry wood chips or pieces of tree bark
- 2 handfuls of dry soil
- A cookie sheet
- 10 roly-poly bugs
- Water

Instructions:

1. Mix the dead leaves, wood chips, and soil together.
2. Divide the mixture into 2 equal piles.
3. Add enough water to 1 pile to make it very damp. Use your hands to spread the moisture evenly through the pile.
4. Place the cookie sheet on a flat surface.

5. Place the damp pile at one end of the cookie sheet. Place the dry pile at the other end. Use your hand to flatten the piles and spread them out a bit.
6. Release the 10 roly-poly bugs onto the cookie sheet between the two piles. Try to place them so they are the same distance from both piles.
7. Observe where they go for about 20 minutes. Try not to breathe on them as you watch.

Conclusion:

How many bugs moved to the damp pile? How many moved to the dry one? How many were still crawling around the cookie sheet? Did any roly-polys try one pile first and then the other? What does this tell you about which pile the roly-polys prefer? Was your hypothesis correct? What is your conclusion?

You probably concluded that roly-poly bugs like damp places.

EXPERIMENT #2

Are Bugs Bugged by Light?

You just learned that roly-poly bugs prefer to live in damp places. What else do you think roly-polys look for in a home? Do you think they like dark places or bright ones? This experiment will help us find out.

Here are two possible hypotheses:

1. Roly-polys like dark places.
2. Roly-polys like bright places.

Let's get started!

Here's what you'll need:

- A large sheet of black construction paper or black plastic.
- A lamp with a bright light
- 2–4 paper towels
- 10 roly-poly bugs
- A cookie sheet
- Water
- Tape

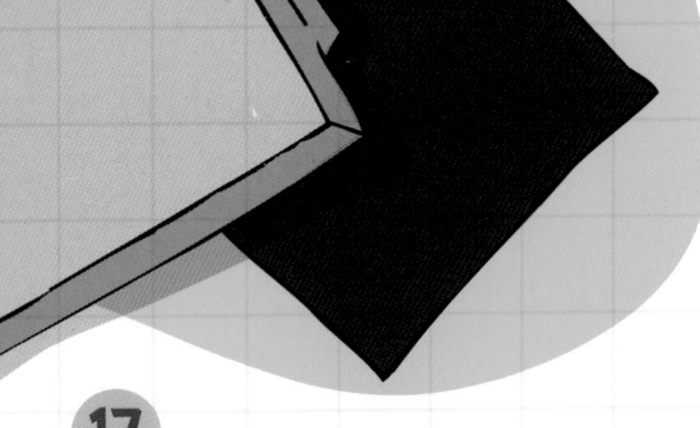

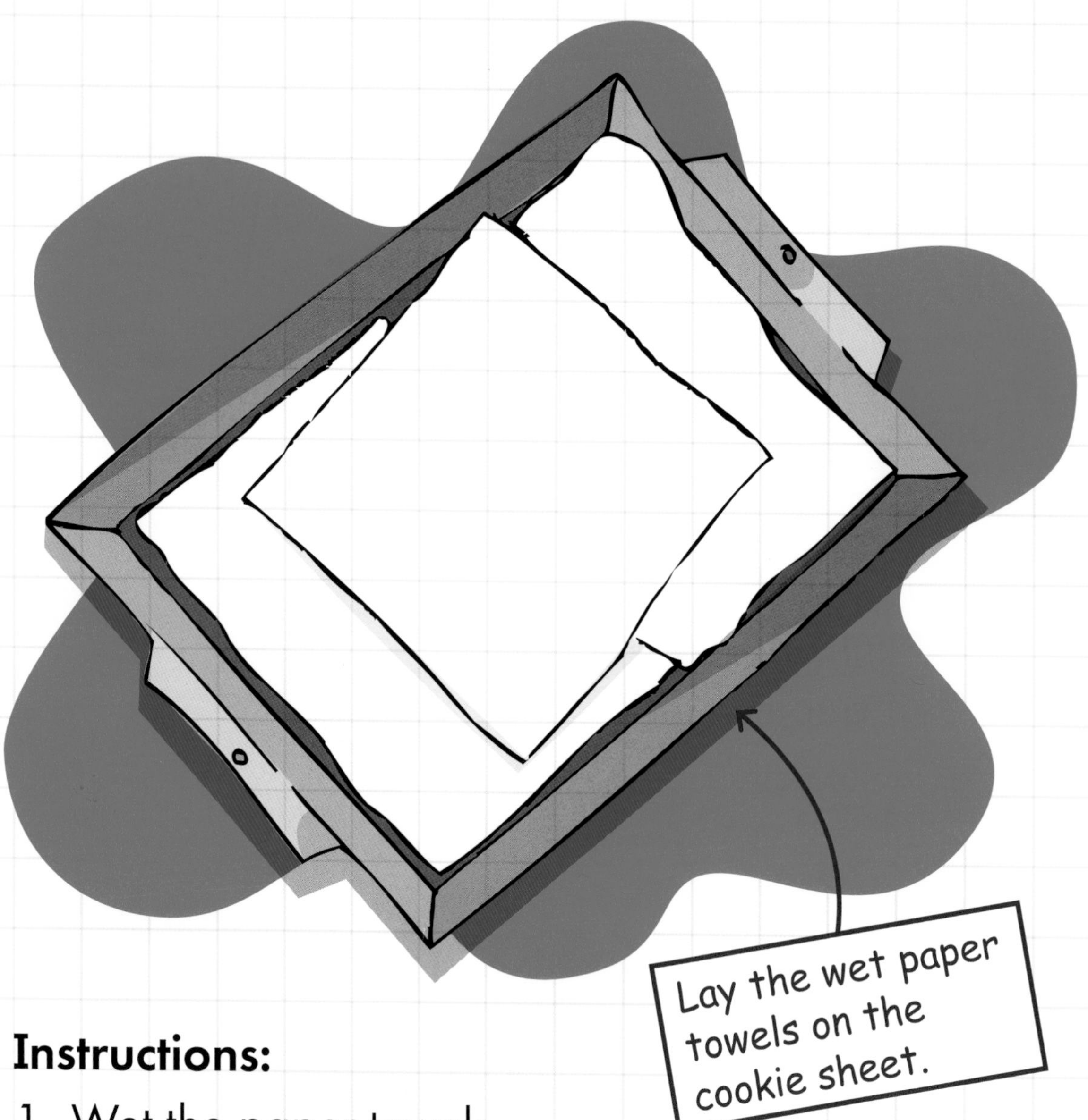

Instructions:

1. Wet the paper towels.
2. Lay the paper towels flat on the cookie sheet so they cover it completely. Remember, the bugs like damp places!

3. Cover the left one-third of the cookie sheet with the black paper or plastic. Tape the edges to the cookie sheet so that the black paper or plastic stays in place. There should be a bit of space between the paper or plastic and the surface of the cookie sheet.

4. Set the cookie sheet near the lamp. The side without paper or plastic should be closest to the lamp.
5. Turn the lamp on. The cookie sheet should now have a bright side and a shaded side. Make sure the bright side is not too hot. This could hurt the bugs. It might also change the results of your experiment.
6. Place the roly-polys on the center of the cookie sheet.

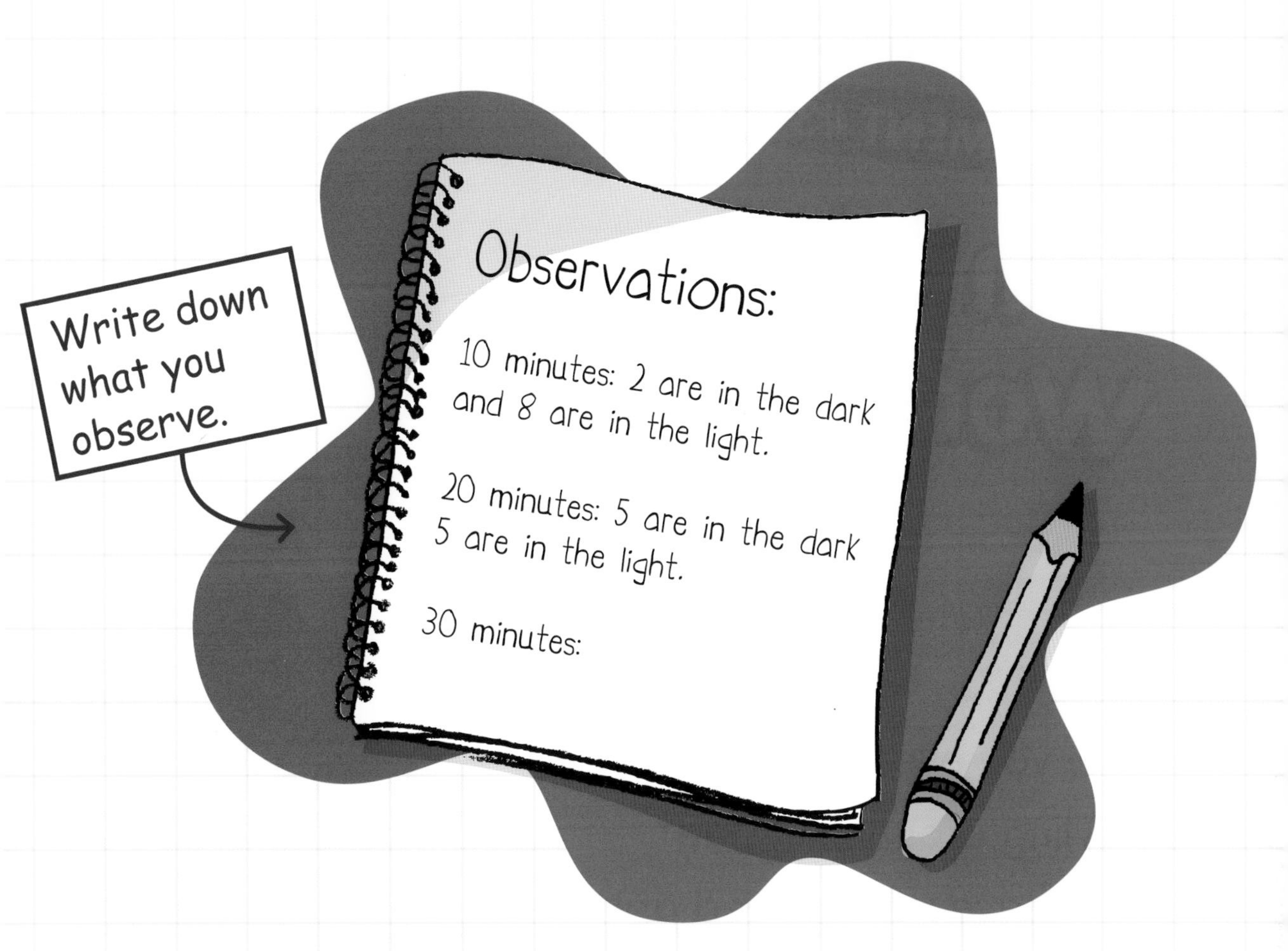

7. Observe their behavior for the next hour. Every 10 minutes, check how many are in the dark area and how many are in the light area. Write down what you see.

Conclusion:

How many roly-polys went to each side of the cookie sheet? What does this tell you? Was your hypothesis correct? What is your conclusion?

EXPERIMENT #3

Which Worms Win?

Have you ever seen worms crawling around outside? What have you noticed about the way they move? Do you think temperature might determine how fast worms move? Let's do an experiment to find out.

Here are some possible hypotheses:

1. Warm worms move more quickly than cold ones.
2. Cold worms move more quickly than warm ones.
3. Temperature does not affect a worm's speed.

Which hypothesis is correct? Let's find out!

Here's what you'll need:

- A mug
- 2 identical dinner plates or pie pans
- A marking pen with washable ink
- An adult helper
- 2 plastic tubs with lids
- 20 mealworms. You can buy mealworms at a pet store.
- A cold place, such as a refrigerator
- A place that is warm, but not hot, such as a sunny windowsill

Instructions:

1. Place the mug upside down in the center of the plate or pan.
2. Use the marking pen to trace a circle around the mug. Lift up the mug. You should see a nearly perfect circle in the center of the plate or pan.
3. Repeat steps 1 and 2 with the other plate or pan.

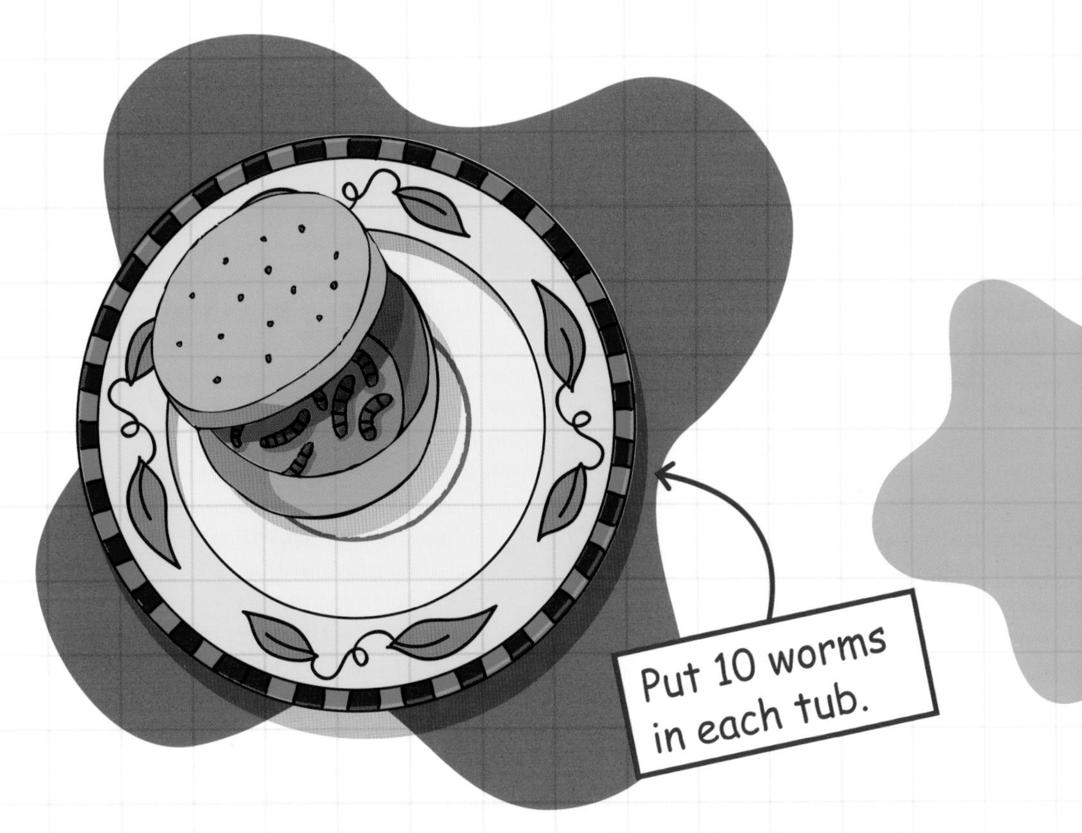

4. Have an adult poke some small air holes in the lids of the margarine tubs.
5. Carefully place 10 mealworms in each tub. Cover the tubs with the lids.
6. Put one tub and one plate in a cold place for 20 minutes. Do not use a freezer!
7. Put the other tub and plate in a warm place for 20 minutes.
8. After 20 minutes, place the cooled and warmed plates side by side. Make sure they are not in direct sunlight.

9. Dump the cold worms into the circle on the cold plate. Do it quickly, but make sure all of the worms go inside the circle.
10. Dump the warm worms into the circle on the warm plate.
11. Observe the worms' movements for the next 10 minutes. How fast do they move?

Conclusion:

How long does it take all the warm worms to leave the circle? How long does it take the cold worms? Which group was faster? Was your hypothesis correct?

You learned that temperature affects how fast mealworms move.

Do It Yourself!

Okay, scientists! You learned that roly-poly bugs prefer to live in damp, dark places. You also learned that temperature affects how fast mealworms move. You learned these things by thinking like scientists.

Do you have some new questions about bugs? Maybe you'd like to know if bugs prefer cold or warm places. You might wonder if bugs like to live in grassy areas. How can you find out? Use the scientific method!

GLOSSARY

conclude (kuhn-KLOOD) to make a final decision based on what you know

conclusion (kuhn-KLOO-zhuhn) a final decision, thought, or opinion

experiment (ecks-PARE-uh-ment) a scientific way to test a guess about something

hypothesis (hy-POTH-uh-sihss) a logical guess about what will happen in an experiment

method (METH-uhd) a way of doing something

observe (ob-ZURV) to see something or notice things by using the other senses

temperature (TEM-pur-uh-chur) a measurement of how hot or cold something is

FOR MORE INFORMATION

BOOKS

Backyard Laboratory. New York: Children's Press, 2008.

Davies, Andrew. *Super-Size Bugs*. New York: Sterling Publishing Co., Inc., 2008.

Hardyman, Robyn. *Bugs*. Redding, CT: Brown Bear Books, 2009.

WEB SITES

Discovery Kids—Put Some Worms to Work
yucky.discovery.com/flash/fun_n_games/activities/activities/activity_worms.html
Find a fun project with worms.

PBS Kids—ZOOMsci: Counting Bugs
pbskids.org/zoom/activities/sci/countingbugs.html
Try a simple activity that will help you learn about bugs in your neighborhood.

Sacramento Zoo—Mealworm to Beetle Project
www.saczoo.com/Page.aspx?pid=441
Learn how to set up a home for mealworms and watch them grow and develop.

INDEX

ABOUT THE AUTHOR

Susan H. Gray has a master's degree in zoology. She has written more than 100 science and reference books for children and especially loves writing about biology. Susan also likes to garden and play the piano. She lives in Cabot, Arkansas, with her husband, Michael, and many pets.